I0799591

WonderWorks

Decodable Reader

Unit 4

McGraw Hill

Contents

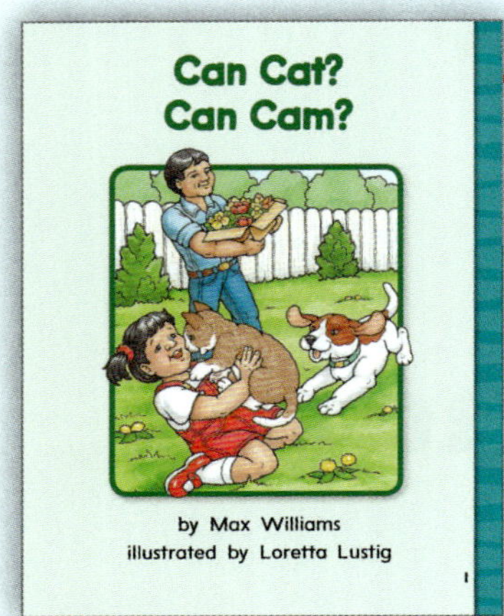
Can Cat?
Can Cam?
by Max Williams
illustrated by Loretta Lustig
1

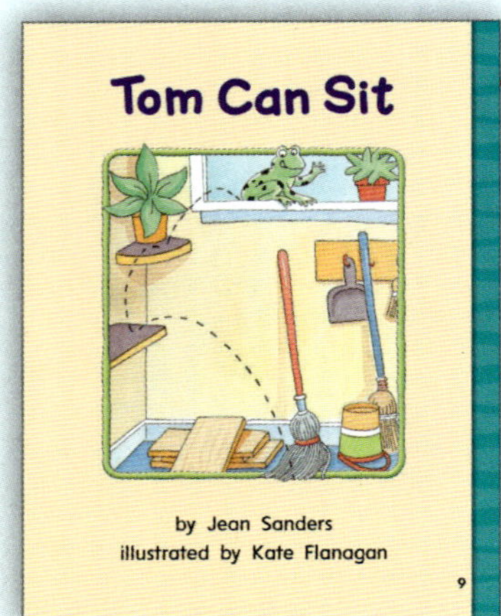
Tom Can Sit
by Jean Sanders
illustrated by Kate Flanagan
9

Dad Did It!
by Denise Fellows
17

Can Cat? Can Cam?

by Max Williams
illustrated by Loretta Lustig

Tan Cat and Cam can **go**.

Cam can **go** in the  .

flowers

Cam can sit in a  .
tub

Tan Cat can **go** in  .

flowers

Tan Cat can sit in a  .

box

Tan Cat can!
Cam can!

Tom Can Sit

by Jean Sanders

illustrated by Kate Flanagan

Can Tom sit on a mop?

Tom can not sit on a mop.

Can Tom  on top?

hop

Tom can not  on top.

hop

Can Tom sit at a  ?

window

Tom can!

You can see Tom sit.

Dad Did It!

White Rock/Getty Images

by Denise Fellows

Maximilian Stock Ltd./Photographer's Choice/Getty Images

Do you like  ?

spaghetti

Asia Images Group/Getty Images

Dad can  it.

cook

ImageSource/age footstock

Dad can  the pot.

fill

Marta Nardini/Flickr/Getty Images

Dad can tip it in.
Dad can tip it in the pot.

Dave King/Dorling Kindersley/Getty Images

Dad can dip, dip, dip.
Dad can dip it on top.

White Rock/Getty Images

We like it!

Unit 4

Word Count: 36

Decodable Words

Target Phonics Element: Initial /k/*c*

Cam, can, cat

Review: *in, sit, tan*

High-Frequency Words

go

Review: *a, and, can, the*

Word Count: 37

Decodable Words

Target Phonics Element: Short *o*

mop, not, on, Tom, top

Review: *at, can, sit*

High-Frequency Words

you

Review: *a, see*

Week 3 • *Dad Did It!*

Word Count: 39

Decodable Words

Target Phonics Element: Initial and Final /d/*d*

Dad, did, dip

Review: *can, in, it, on, pot, tip*

High-Frequency Words

do

Review: *like, the, we, you*

Decoding skills taught to date:

Consonants /m/*m*, /s/*s*, /p/*p*, /t/*t*; Short *a*; Short *i*; Initial and Final /n/*n*; Initial /k/*c*; Short *o*; Initial and Final /d/*d*